DESTINATION
CANYON COUNTRY
THE NATURAL WONDERS OF
ARIZONA AND UTAH

Canyonlands National Park: a bend in the Colorado River beneath Dead Horse Point.

DESTINATION
CANYON COUNTRY

THE NATURAL WONDERS OF
ARIZONA AND UTAH

Photographs: Helmut Friedrich
Text: Witold Sartorius
Helmut Friedrich

WINDSOR BOOKS
INTERNATIONAL

A view of Monument Valley from Hunt's Mesa on the Colorado Plateau.

CONTENTS

Windows Section in Arches National Park, Utah.

CANYON COUNTRY: ARIZONA AND UTAH

The Land and Its People: How It All Began

On 24 May 1869 Major John Wesley Powell, a researcher and traveller, set out with a company of nine adventurers to explore the course of the Colorado River and its canyons. It was the first systematic attempt to investigate the wild and forbidding expanses of the American southwest. Some decades previous, for completely different motives, European trophy hunters had already pushed into the area now occupied by the states of Arizona and Utah, with its fascinating deserts and canyons, its evergreen forests and steep, heavily eroded peaks and cliffs. Between 1821 and 1848, when the land was still officially part of Mexico but actually populated by Navajo, Hopi, Apaches and other untouched native tribes, white hunters and trappers from the east criss-crossed the area in search of prey. And with them, unawares, came a new age which would soon put an end to the harmony that reigned between man and nature in this part of the world.

Here, over unimaginably vast expanses of time, the forces of nature fashioned a unity of worlds both in macrocosm and microcosm. Today, however, this unity has been summarily torn apart by artificial borders. We must try to ignore these borders if we want to breathe the air of this world as it used to be long, long ago when man lived in communion with nature. One of these artificial lines is the southern border of Arizona, drawn in the aftermath of the American invasion that by 1848 had cost Mexico half of its territory. To appreciate the unity of this landscape we should probably start our journey at the Gulf of California. Here begins that range of mountains that robs the Pacific breezes of their moisture, thereby producing one of the world's most unusual landscapes: the Sonora Desert. Cut off from the Pacific by the southern foothills of the Sierra Nevada Mountains, this desert begins on the peninsula known as Baja California and extends through the Mexican state of Sonora and far into Arizona. Wide-open vistas and sun-parched depressions separated by sinuous mountains ranges char-

acterize this region. The geological history of Arizona and Utah goes back more than 1,700 million years to the Pre-Cambrian period, when North America drifted to the southeast and collided with another part of the earth's crust. Cliffs at the edge of the plates were crushed; new ones were thrust up by the mighty force of the impact. At the juncture of this gigantic geological disaster there arose a mighty mountain range, just as the Himalayas were created when the Indian subcontinent collided with Asia.

The Sonora Desert is bordered to the north by central highlands. Geologically, this is a transitional zone situated between the deserts to the south and the Colorado Plateau. Here the mountains are higher and join into cohesive ranges with the same northwest-to-southeast trend as the stretches of desert. The plains and basins are narrower and less deep; the rocks that fill them are less weathered than in the arid expanses further to the south. Only the more exposed cliffs and peaks have been polished by wind and furrowed by water falling in the short but violent rainstorms.

The first white man to reach the southern edge of the abyss later known as the Grand Canyon was a fortune hunter, Garcia Lopez de Cardenas. After months of searching for the legendary "Seven Cities of Cibola" he encountered the same bizarre view that even today continues to astonish visitors from far and near. The overwhelming vista goes far beyond anything captured in paintings or photographs. The Grand Canyon of the Colorado River is one of the mightiest and most breathtaking spectacles on earth. It forms the heartland of the Colorado Plateau, a landscape full of elevated plains rising over 9,000 feet/3,000 metres above sea level. And these plains are rent and fissured by canyons.

Here, for 600 million years, a large piece of the earth's crust remained intact. It is still recognizable today. The differences in landscape between the plateau and the elevated plains bear witness to a geological diversity that mirrors the evolution of our planet. Beneath the Colorado Plateau the earth's crust is thicker and the heat from the planet's interior is less

The solitary Delicate Arch in Arches National Park, held by many to be the most beautiful of its kind in the world. The park can boast of more than ninety of these natural wonders.

than in the surrounding regions. Small earthquakes occur sporadically on the western border, which extends far into Utah to the base of the Wasatch Rocky Mountains. Today, this is the most heavily populated area in Utah. The northern part of central Utah has a strip of arable land 160 miles/250 kilometres wide extending north and south of the Wasatch Rockies.

"We believe...that Zion will be erected upon this continent." Thus wrote Joseph Smith, the founder of the much persecuted, long-suffering and ultimately triumphant utopian religious movement known as the "Church of Jesus Christ of Latter Day Saints" or, more familiarly, as the Mormons. Fleeing persecution in the eastern United States, the Mormons came to Utah in 1847, and have dominated its history ever since. Hard-working, self-sacrificing and disciplined, they fulfilled an Old Testament prophecy by literally "making the desert bloom". The society they erected was a theocratic system in which the elders of the church also wielded political power. This soon brought them into grave conflict with the United States Congress. One Mormon custom in particular – polygamy, the taking of many wives – remained a bone of contention until 1890, when it was renounced by the head of the church. Not until 1896 was Utah admitted to the Union. Since then, Mormon missionaries have plied their faith throughout the world (with the exception of black Africa), and their once exclusive church continues to gain adherents. It has always remained conservative and continues as ever to exclude black-skinned peoples from full membership.

Even today Arizona remains the "Indian State". It was here that resistance to the white intruders lasted the longest. Arizona's Indians – or native Americans as they are properly called – fought innumerable bloody battles until 1886, when the last of their heroes, the Apache chieftain Geronimo, was forced to capitulate. Later the Indians were consigned to reservations, which still make up a large part of Arizona's territory.

The first humans to settle in this part of North America arrived about 3,000 years ago. However, they did not remain. Not until the first half of the first millennium did permanent settlements arise. Hashk'aan Ts'osi, a Navajo, recalls: "Yes, there was a people that became the Anasazi, the Old Tribe. But now all you can see of them is the ruins of their buildings. Over there, where the sand is, you can still find broken bits and pieces … That's the way it is, everywhere, even as far as Utah. Wherever you go the broken pots and stones and signs of the Anasazi were there before you.

Devils Garden in Arches National Park, Utah, as seen through Partition Arch.

You can see that there were very many of them and that they jostled each other as the Navajo do today. What made them go away? Maybe the sacred things they lived for. Nothing can survive by itself. It's the same with sheep and horses: if there's no rain they die. The Anasazi went away, and we Navajo came."

The Anasazi culture lasted almost one thousand years and has fascinated archaeologists to the present day. Around the year 1300, for unknown reasons, it perished within a space of no more than fifty years, leaving behind its cultural achievements, the ruins known as the pueblo culture. When the Spaniards came they found other peoples, particularly the Hopi and Navajo, who had adopted from their predecessors a love of turquoise and the art of building pueblos. The Indians lived in harmony with nature; the land was their destiny. They accumulated an immense body of knowledge on plants and animals, the living deities who governed their religious life. They viewed the world as a "hogan", an area where the whole of life unfolds and whose pillars are the mountain peaks. Today, we white rulers of the earth have rediscovered this world view. We call it ecology. The white men came to conquer. Driven by a lust for gold, silver and land, they slit the bellies of the mountains to look for metal, and populated the land in order to seize possession of it.

Eventually the gold diggers left; the farmers and ranchers, however, remained. Of the former we can still see the ruins of their buildings. Countless and once flourishing towns vanished overnight. Often their very names betray the reason for their existence and downfall: "Goldroad", "Goldfield", "Silverbelt", "Oro Blanco", "Nugget". As the precious metals were depleted the population moved on. For ranchers and farmers, water is more important than land. Land is worthless without water, and only by means of irrigation could Arizona and Utah consolidate the foundations of their economic growth. The centuries-old irrigation canals of the Hohokam Indians are still in use today.

One of the largest water reservoirs on the continent, technology that led to the invention of air conditioning, a booming economy: today these factors attract many people to Arizona. Arizona has evolved from an agricultural and mining state into a centre of industry and high technology. This is why the urban centres of Phoenix and Tucson emerged and continue to expand. Americans even have a special term for life in Arizona: "oasis civilization".

Blue Skies and Sunswept Plains: the Desert

The huge arid expanse that extends from the northern half of Sonora in Mexico to the southern half of Arizona will fascinate anyone with an eye for the desert. It is hot and very arid: its potential annual evaporation is higher than its annual rainfall. Yet only in the remote southwest corner of Arizona, in Yuma County along the border to California, are there any dunes. Water, of course, is in short supply. But the extreme climate has given rise to a wide array of flora and fauna whose survival tactics will astonish the observant visitor. This natural balance, created over a period of millennia, is extremely sensitive and fragile. The many national parks, national monuments and other kinds of nature reserves bear witness to this fragility. At the least, they provide a few enclaves where nature can still unfold its beauties in their original purity.

The size of the Sonora Desert can be defined geologically. But the area it covers contains a very wide variety of habitats for plants and animals. Completely different forms of life can be discovered in its fiery steppe-like plains, its sand dunes and its shady canyons. Perhaps the most famous species of plant in Arizona and Sonora is the saguaro cactus. It is found only here and, almost symbolically, in almost every Western film ever made. Shaped like columns, these plants, growing in groups, dominate the landscape. Despite their large size and robust appearance, they are very sensitive and will grow only where they find exactly the conditions they need. This has limited their expansion to the southern part of Arizona and the northern area of Sonora in Mexico. To the west, in California, and east of Tucson they are almost nowhere to be seen. The Sonora Desert has the necessary summer rainfall and enough warmth to allow the seeds of the saguaro to germinate. Just how sensitively these cacti react to differences of temperature can be seen in the canyons of Arizona, where large colonies of saguaro grow on the hot southern slopes but only very few on the cooler northern sides. Only once in its life does this plant sprout two inconspicuous leaves: when the seed germinates and the young plant begins to grow in the sheltering shadow of a tree or shrub.

In spite of their many natural enemies both small and large, such as ants, desert rats and birds, the saguaro colonies would still be living in balance with the environment if – always the same old story – man had not entered the scene. Although it is strictly forbidden to damage these plants, the "gentle giants" on the wayside paths are used again and again by drunken tourists or high-spirited teenagers as targets for spears, arrows and guns. Some attempt to show off their muscles by toppling a saguaro. Its widespread but shallow roots offer little resistance, and the "heroic deed" is soon accomplished.

Today, the most beautiful specimens of this plant are found in the nature reserves and national monuments around Tucson in southern Arizona and near the border to Mexico. Park rangers ensure that their natural surroundings remain largely intact. Where they do exist they are far and away the largest "trees" around, and as such much exploited by other living creatures. The gila woodpecker and the gilded flicker – both native to the Sonora Desert – build their nests in the trunk of these giants, and when they move to another nest there is a long list of prospective new tenants. One of the most interesting of these, scarcely larger than an ordinary sparrow, is the microathene owl. The male searches for an abandoned woodpecker nest, and when it has found a suitable one it asks the approval of the female. Microathene owls are migrating birds that appear in the cactus forests in late spring. They hunt at night, and reveal a culinary preference for large beetles and moths, scorpions and other smaller animals.

The Sonora Desert harbours a rich kingdom of living beings. Many less celebrated species of cactus rim its mountainsides or grow on its plains. Some of them might even be mistaken for flowering trees or shrubs. Only at close range do their putative flowers turn out to be myriad groups of hair-thin prickles refracting the rays of the sun. But these arid wastes are more than a home for cacti, insects and birds. Mammals can also be found here. Visitors are most likely to notice the antelope ground squirrels. These lithe, silver-grey animals are living proof that survival in the desert is not always a question of specialization, but can be just the opposite. Some species of ground squirrels living in Arizona's deserts, for example, will literally eat anything: flowers, cactus seeds, insects – there is practically nothing they don't relish. In this way they can find nourishment throughout the year. And when they go underground it is not to hibernate during the dry winter but rather to escape the blistering heat of the day or the night-time chill for a short while. In other words, we stand a good chance of watching them go about their daily rounds. This is much more difficult in the case of the wood rat, another typical denizen of the desert. The wood rat takes its name from its habit of biting off twigs and putting them into a pile under which it builds its nest. In this respect it resembles a beaver, and in fact the wood rat is known as a sort of "desert beaver". It hunts at night and drags into its house anything that looks tast, even if it is part of your camping equipment. Another animal typical of the region is the kangaroo rat, the preferred quarry of the kit fox.

Sun's Eye in Monument Valley, formed by a small stone arch. The contrast of colours and the interplay of light and shade give this valley its sublime charm.

Among reptiles, the most famous is the rattlesnake, whose name alone sends shivers down many a spine. In fact, as experienced desert-lovers well know, its reputation is undeserved. When the Spaniards arrived in Arizona they were fascinated by this "snake with the bell" and gave it the name "cascabel", meaning not only bell but also the knob at the end of a cannon. Unfortunately, our image of snakes has been tainted by too many horror stories and half-truths. They are neither slippery nor slimy, nor do they lust for opportunities to ambush innocent tourists. Instead, they are shy and slip into hiding at the slightest vibration of the ground that might announce the approach of a man or large animal. If you come too close to a rattlesnake it will "rattle" the end of its tail. Its bite, which can be fatal even to humans, is used to stun its prey, which consists mainly of small mammals such as kangaroo rats. Like all other living beings, snakes perform a vital function in the ecology of the desert. It's best to let them be.

Although many of Arizona's desert dwellers can still be found throughout the state, their habitat is increasingly being encroached upon by humans. This lends special importance to the national parks and nature reserves. In a certain sense even the Indian reservations help preserve the balance of the ecology, for life still goes on there fairly much in traditional, environmentally sound ways. Still, the Indian lifestyle is vanishing at a shocking speed. In the hands of the white man, many of these once proud lords of the land have become alcoholic welfare cases. It is no exaggeration to say that in the midst of the United States one can find worse living conditions than in many countries of the so-called Third World. But the beauty of the landscape on these reservations and the culture of their inhabitants still warrant a visit. The craftsmanship of the Navajo is world famous, displayed in their magnificent blankets and splendid silver jewelry.

Before we turn to one of the mightiest geological wonders of the world – the Grand Canyon of the Colorado River – we should pause at the giant meteor crater on the road leading from Flagstaff to Albuquerque, New Mexico. Today it lies in a barren expanse recalling a moonscape – which may explain why this area was used as a training field for the Apollo astronauts before their moon landing. The crater is the best preserved of its kind, resembling those on the moon and other bodies in our solar system. It was created about 22,000 years ago when an iron meteorite of some 60,000 tons plunged to the earth's surface.

Magic in Rock: the Grand Canyon

Despite their fascinating flora and fauna, the two "mountain states" of Arizona and Utah are mainly a wonderland for geology buffs. This becomes immediately apparent as we peer down into the depths and breadth of the Grand Canyon, a masterpiece of nature and a open book on the history of the earth. In its nethermost depths we find primordial sediments and volcanic rocks that have been crushed, pulverized and reshifted over millions of years. Today they tell us about early conditions on our planet – about the birth of mighty mountain ranges and their disappearance after thousands upon thousands of years of erosion by water and wind. The walls of the Grand Canyon are laid out like a geology textbook: the oldest rock formations and sediments are at the bottom, and every step upwards brings us to a newer layer in time. The hard crystalline rock far below at the river originated an inconceivably long time ago – about two billion years. It is visible in the eastern part of the valley, where most of the Canyon's visitors can be found. The granite rock was then buried under a mass of younger stone about twelve miles/twenty kilometres thick. This was later washed away by erosion, leaving the primordial

granite on the surface awaiting new deposits. The next layer is formed of Pre-Cambrian rock about one billion years old, containing traces of the living beings that peopled the seas at that time. At the end of the Pre-Cambrian Period there began a long epoch of erosion, ending in the formation of a Cambrian sea occupying virtually the whole of what is now the Colorado Plateau. Here lived many species of sponges, corals, trilobites and other animals whose shells and traces can be seen in the limestone deposits of this period. New stages of erosion and sedimentation followed, as did new incursions of the ocean. All these events left behind tell-tale marks in the form of geological layers which can be read by experts "like an open book".

But how did the Colorado River produce such a gigantic trench? Originally the river flowed southward from Utah, as it does today. But it continued by running straight to Arizona, to the bed of the river known today as the Little Colorado, before reaching a great ocean in the eastern part of the state. To the west there arose a different drainage system that gradually ate its way eastward by erosion. The wall of rock separating the two rivers became thinner and thinner. Eventually the two rivers broke through, and the waters of the Colorado rushed into the new, steeper river bed.

Swollen by the heavy rainstorms of the ice ages, the river grew in size and developed its boundless strength. The result was the Grand Canyon as we know it today. This process of erosion still continues, but at a much slower pace since the flow of the Colorado has been blocked by dams and the primordial granite of the present-day river bed offers more resistance than the soft rock above. Today, then, the Grand Canyon is becoming wider rather than deeper.

The early pioneers in northern Arizona and southern Utah faced the virtually insurmountable task of trying to overcome the natural barrier of the Grand Canyon and its tributaries. For all their beauty, the mighty gorges of the Colorado were not likely to impress early settlers, most of them Mormons from the north, who were more likely to regard them as God's curse on their way to the "Promised Land". The few known crossings were spread over the entire length of the Grand Canyon and were very dangerous for horses and covered wagons. One of the most important was Pierce Ferry to the west of the canyon, not far from present-day Lake Mead. Another relatively easy crossing was in Hite in Utah, at the mouth of the Dirty Devil River, but this involved a journey of 300 miles/ 500 kilometres and the same distance back again on the other side. Around 1850 another crossing was discovered, one which had already been used in the 1770s by Padre Silvestre Veley de Escalante. It soon became a major transportation axis, especially once a ferry service – Lee's Ferry – had been set up at the mouth of the Paria River. Mormon settlers tried several times to cross the river about 120 miles/200 kilometres upstream, lowering and hoisting their freight and equipment over cliffs hundreds of feet high. But they soon abandoned the project, and Lee's Ferry became the favourite crossing. Here, thanks to a confluence of hard and soft layers of rock, there were a number of gentle valleys leading to Marble Canyon, an extension of the Grand Canyon. The heavy conestogas of the pioneers could easily roll down to the ferry or be pulled in the opposite direction by horses. This "ramp" can still be seen at the point where today's adventurers lower their big rubber rafts and set out on the long journey through the Canyon.

Even today this journey still smacks of a voyage of discovery. But no one who conquers this once perilous river nowadays can appreciate the stark fear felt by Major Powell and his companions. His first expedition – three small wooden boats in all – passed this point on 5 August 1869 on his journey into the depths of these secretive gorges. Today, thanks to the courage and stamina of these men – and the others who took part in Powell's second expedition of 1872 – the Colorado and its tributaries have been largely explored. The dam at Glen Canyon makes it possible to control the volume of water directed into the river, and thus predicts the dangers of the journey. Still, even with the conveniences of modern-today technology, a boat trip through the Grand Canyon is one of the greatest adventures in our civilized world.

But this part of the earth has many other beauties of nature to offer besides the Grand Canyon. To the east lies another nature reserve, Petrified Forest National Park. The major part of it is occupied by the Painted Desert, which takes its name from the brilliant colours shining through the eroded surfaces of the badlands. These colours are the result of mineral impurities, in particular metal oxides, producing the various hues of red, brown, blue and yellow.

The main attraction of the park, however, is its giant petrified trees. Even today, millions of years later, we can still note the delicacy of their cell structures and count their annual rings. Water-soluble quartz was responsible for turning this timber into stone. The trees grew 200 million years ago in the damp, humid swamps of the Triassic Period. After dying of disease, fire or insect damage, they were swept to their present location by the swirling masses of water. The volcanic ash of the Triassic Period contained silicon. This dissolved in water, and the trees absorbed the solution, which, in high concentration, caused quartz crystals to form in the cells of the wood. After a while the quartz also penetrated the cell walls. Regaining its crystalline form, it preserved the structure of the wood in minute detail. Here, too, the brilliant colours of the tree trunks are the result of mineral impurities in the quartz.

God's Country: Utah

Geological time in the southern and central parts of Utah began 225 million years ago. The arid plateaus, furrowed by gorges such as Bryce Canyon or Zion Canyon, are famous for their unique scenery. Today's visitors to Zion National Park are no less impressed than the first Mormon settlers by its stone pillars and its conglomerations of rocks in the shape of cathedrals. No doubt this is why the pious immigrants gave it the name "Zion". This spectacular scene of erosion is a product of very recent geological events. The key to its origins lies in the sequence of sedimentation and subsequent periods of erosion immortalized in the canyon walls. Now a desert region located nearly 7,000 feet/2,000 metres above sea level, Zion Canyon did not always look as it does today. During the early Triassic Period it was flooded many times, producing shallow oceans upon whose seabeds were deposited many thin layers

Spider Rock in Canyon de Chelly National Monument, living proof that rock formations can take on huge proportions. This needle is as tall as the Empire State Building.

17

Left Mitten, Right Mitten and Merrick Butte in Monument Valley. The tops of these buttes show the former altitude of the Colorado Plateau.

of gypsum, lime and sandstone. These formations are displayed to best advantage in the red, brown, pink and grey cliffs of the southwestern section of the park, along the Virgin River. The next period of erosion left behind an uneven, furrowed landscape which was then covered by a sediment consisting of variegated sand and pebbles. In the late Triassic Period the Zion region was a flat plain with broad rivers and shallow freshwater lakes. It was then that coloured sandstone conglomerates were superimposed on the earliest layers. Here we can find many fossils, including skeletons of reptiles, traces of freshwater shellfish, and much petrified wood.

At the beginning of the Jurassic Period the climate abruptly changed, giving rise to an arid landscape with mighty sand dunes not unlike the present-day Sahara. It is these petrified, "frozen" dunes that make up the largest part of the spectacular Navajo sandstone formations – stone promontories of grey, brown or red, hundreds of feet high. The most striking feature of these sandstones is their so-called "cross deposits", a pattern also observable on sand dunes in shifting winds. As the Zion dunes turned into stone they retained this cross-hatch pattern. Not only does it add to the beauty of these formations, it also provides valuable information that helps us reconstruct the geological history of Utah.

If Zion's rocks are ancient and primeval, the landscape itself came about more recently. There have been various attempts to explain the origins of this type of canyon, with its flat bottom and dizzyingly steep walls. But it was not a mighty earthquake nor a glacier, but rather the inconspicuous Virgin River that gave this region its present appearance. How was it possible for such a relatively small river to create such a bizarre canyon? Only by a combination of factors. At the end of the Tertiary Period there occurred several shifts that lifted the southern section of Utah from sea level to an altitude of nearly 10,000 feet/3,000 metres. This had two important consequences. For one, this upward movement broke the earth's crust, creating many fissures which were at first invisible. Moreover, the speed of the rivers – and thus their powers of erosion – increased dramatically as a result of the steeper incline. This is what gave such enormous force to a river as small as the Virgin. Even today about 300,000 tons of material are washed annually out of the canyon! Most of the energy is consumed in deepening the river bed; the canyon itself is widening at a very much slower pace. This accounts for Zion's high, steep cliffs. The most spectacular spot to view the disproportion between its breadth and height is at the Narrows. Here, separated by just a few yards, the walls ascend hundreds of feet.

The flora and fauna of Zion Park reveal the influence not only of the arid desert climate but also of the Rocky Mountains. We can find yucca palms, various types of cactus and other desert plants, but also countless species of wildflowers and, in moist areas, maple trees. The largest animal to be seen is the mountain goat. There are also many small mammals such as chipmunks and coyotes, not to mention reptiles.

The southern section of Utah has always been sparsely populated. Thus, large parts of the landscape are still virgin, and national parks were established to ensure that they will remain so. This applies as well to the second natural wonder of the state – Bryce Canyon National Park. Strictly speaking, it is not a canyon at all, for it is shaped like a horseshoe, forming a natural amphitheatre. This mighty depression – about three miles/five kilometres long, one mile/one-and-a-half-kilometres wide and hundreds of feet deep – was hewn from weathered rock by the forces of nature. Its geological formations are fascinating and almost limitless: pillars, cliffs, natural bridges, arches and windows. Often the rocks look like ruined castles or temples. Bryce Canyon likewise went through several periods of sedimentation and erosion. But in this case the crucial factor was physical and chemical weathering rather than the erosive powers of water and wind. "Physical" weathering means that the rock was broken down directly by physical forces, especially frost and the living strength of plants, whose roots grow into the cracks and burst the stone. Substances in rainwater, particularly acids, trigger chemical reactions and dissolve parts of the rock. The monumental landscape is made up of the parts left behind.

But what caused these remains to assume such striking shapes? The answer lies in the composition of the rock itself. The entire canyon consists of layers of rock with different amounts of resistance to the forces of weathering, creating the type of landscape that greets the eye in Bryce Canyon. The softer sedimentary parts erode more quickly, leaving behind gullies, fissures and recesses of various sizes, while the harder limestone layers form the banks and promontories as well as the "heads" on the pillars. Moreover, many of the walls are permeated with cracks and potential fault lines which, in the course of time, give rise to arches and "windows". At a more advanced stage of weathering this results in long rows of pointed, obelisk-like sculptures of the sort we find in Silent City. The same forces of nature that gave birth to these bizarre forms are also bent on their destruction. But by the time the remnants of the old formations have been permanently swept aside into the valley, their replacements will already have appeared at the rim of the canyon.

White House Ruins in Canyon de Chelly bear impressive witness to a lost Indian culture. This settlement was built between the eleventh and thirteenth centuries. Its architects, the Anasazi, disappeared with hardly a trace. Even the present-day "tenants", the Pueblo Indians, can tell us nothing about them.

The Grand Canyon in Arizona, the most famous canyon on earth, probably created by the Colorado River.

Sacred Datura, a poisonous member of the nightshade famil. Only at first glance is Canyon Country devoid of vegetation.

TALES OF THE WILD WEST
Eyewitness Accounts and Commentaries on Canyon Country

The fear which must have accompanied Major John Powell and his crew as they ventured down the Green and Colorado Rivers, then uncharted and unexplored territory, was, we hope, greatly alleviated by the awe-inspiring wonders encountered along their route. Eager nineteenth century settlers crossing the Arizona and Utah Territories have left colourful memoirs of their hardships and experiences, while early geographical survey teams provided the details to guide later groups in the expansion and development of the American Southwest. Through the eyes of these writers, the beauty and perils of Canyon Country are here unfolded, be it during a mule ride down to the floor of the Grand Canyon or an encounter with the region's original residents, the American Indians. While most of the texts reflect the wonders of the untamed wilderness, critical voices are also sounded along with a warning, to not attempt to harness or tamper with nature's fragile balance which has evolved through the centuries.

The Great Shell of Kintyel

Nahoditahe told them that he could drive the sickness away with a night chant. "I will lead the dancers," he said, "but I must be dressed in a particular way. I must have strings of fine beads – shell and turquoise – enough to cover my legs and forearms completely, and enough to go around my neck so that I cannot bend my head back. Lastly I must have the largest shell in Kintyel to hang on my back. Four days from now I will be ready to perform the night chant and drive the sickness away."

On the next day the chiefs brought him beads of shell and turquoise, the finest they could collect among all the people, and on the second day they brought him

24

several large shell basins from which to choose to wear upon his back. He measured the shells with his arms as the Wind spirit had told him to do, but his hands joined easily. "None of these is large enough," he said, and they brought him larger and larger shells. Each time they tried to persuade him that the shells were the largest they had, but Nahoditahe rejected all.

On the last day, with much reluctance, they brought him the great shell of Kintyel, and when he clasped it in his arms his fingers did not meet on the opposite side. "This," he said, "is the shell I must wear when I dance."

That evening Nahoditahe ordered them to build a great circle of pine branches, such as the Navahos now build for the rites of their mountain chant. As darkness fell, a great crowd gathered in the enclosure, and fires were lighted around the circle.

Nahoditahe now put on his robe of plumes, covered his arms and legs and neck with the rich beads of the Pueblos, and fastened the great shell of Kintyel upon his back. He led the dancers out into the circle and began to dance. As he danced, he chanted a song about the rising up of white, blue, yellow, and black corn.

This seemed a strange song to the Pueblo people, and they all wondered what it could mean. They soon found out what it meant. To their great astonishment the dancing Navaho began rising slowly from the ground. First his head and then his shoulders rose above the heads of the crowd. Soon his chest and waist lifted above them, but not until his whole body had risen above the level of their heads did they begin to realize the loss that threatened them.

Nahoditahe was rising toward the sky with the great shell of Kintyel and all the wealth of many Pueblos in shell-beads and turquoise. They screamed wildly to him to come down again, but the more they shouted the higher he rose. A dark cloud had formed above him in the starlit sky, and from it lightning streaked beneath his feet. The gods were lifting him to the Upper World. In desperation the people of Kintyel threw ropes up to seize and pull him back to earth, but he was beyond reach of their longest rope. The chiefs shouted for arrows to shoot him down, but before one could be fixed to a bow the Navaho was lost to sight in the black cloud.

Not since that day has the great shell of Kintyel been seen upon this earth. The old men say that it is in one of the pueblos of the Upper World, closely guarded by the War-Eagles of Kinniki.

At the end of the nineteenth and the beginning of the twentieth century, dedicated folklore collectors realized that many Indian tales which had been passed orally through the centuries, from storyteller to storyteller, would be lost forever unless they were written down. Washington Matthews of the American Folklore Society lead this monumental project. This Navajo tale, a myth surrounding the rite of the mountain chant, was told to Matthews by Tall Chanter in the 1890s.

An Encounter with the Indians

On leaving this lake we continued oar journey towards the head waters of the Colerado, which stream empties into the Gulf of Calafornia. After a tedious, but not unpleasant tramp of several days we came to a beautiful situation on one of the main feeders of this river, where we halted to make preparations to spend the winter – it now being about the middle of November. We had remained here but a few days, during which time we were occupied in building tents, &c, for winter, when we were visited by a party of 70 or 80 Indian warriors. These Indians manifested the best of friendship towards us, while in our camp, and said they were going to war with the Snake Indians – whose country we were now in – and they also said they belonged to the Crew nation on the East side of the mountains. In all the intercourse had with them, while they were with us, not the least symptom of deception was discovered, and they parted with us manifesting as much regret as if we had been old acquaintances. But we were doomed to experience the faith of the Crow nation – for, on the same night of their departure, they returned and stole five of our best hunting horses. This was a serious loss to us, and a valuable prize for them – for an Indian belonging to these hunting and warring tribes is poor indeed if he is not the owner of a horse, as it is upon this animal they much depend for success in chasing the buffaloe, and upon him greatly depends the fate of the battle.

ZENAS LEONARD left Pennsylvania in the spring of 1830 and embarked on an expedition across the Rocky Mountains, serving as the clerk to the company. Leonard initially sent letters to his parents, the last being posted from the last white settlement. He returned home unannounced and unexpectedly in the fall of 1835. When he was beset by crowds of anxious enquirers, he threatened to leave again for the West in order to escape the questioning.

A Friendly Conversation

Finally we concluded we did not come out into that wild country to be afraid of a few gunshots, and determined to put on a bold front, fight if we had to, run away if we could not do any better, and take our chances on getting scalped or roasted. Just then we came in sight of three Indian lodges just a little back from the river, and now we knew for certain who had the guns. McMahon and I were in the lead as usual, and it was only a moment before one of the Indians appeared, gun in hand, and made motions for us to come on shore. A cottonwood tree lay nearly across the river, and I had gone so far that I had to go around it and land below, but the other boys behind were afraid to do otherwise than to land right there as the Indian kept his gun lying across his arm. I ran our canoe below to a patch of willows, where we landed and crawled through the brush till we came in sight of the other boys, where we stood and waited a moment to see how they fared, and whether our red men were friends or enemies. There were no suspicious movements on their part, so we came out and walked right up to them. There was some little talk, but I am sure we did not understand one another's language, and so we made motions and they made motions, and we got along better. We went with them down to the tepee, and there we heard the first word that was at all like English and that was "Mormonee," with a sort of questioning tone. Pretty soon one said "Buffalo," and then we concluded they were on a big hunt of some sort. They took us into their lodges and showed us blankets, knives, and guns, and then, with a suggestive motion, said all was "Mormonee," by which we understood they had got them from the Mormons. The Indian in the back part of the lodge looked very pleasant and this countenance showed a good deal of intelligence for a man of the mountains. I now told the boys that we were in a position where we were dependent on some one, and that I had seen enough to convince me that these Indians were perfectly friendly with the Mormons, and that for our own benefit we had better pass ourselves off for Mormons, also. So we put our right hand to our breast and said "Mormonee," with a cheerful countenance, and that act conveyed to them the belief that we were chosen disciples of the great and only Brigham and we became friends at once, as all acknowledged. The fine-looking Indian who sat as king in the lodge now, by motions and a word or two, made himself known as Chief Walker, and when I knew this I took great pains to cultivate his acquaintance.

WILLIAM LEWIS MANLEY was a trapper in Wisconsin when he caught the gold fever of the mid-nineteenth century. He joined up with the Sand Walking Company, a wagon train in Utah; the group consisted of one hundred-seventy wagons and almost five hundred horses and cattle. En route, the troop was overtaken by

...times they seem as thin as paper: the Fisher Towers, majestic and bizarre rock formations about twenty-five miles/ forty kilometres east of Moab, Utah.

Goosenecks State Reserve, where the San Juan River meanders its way through this archaic landscape of narrow bends (goosenecks).

another wagon train with a map showing a short cut to California. Those who broke away from the main trail found themselves in a great dry basin and succumbed to thirst, hunger and exhaustion, forming one of the most dramatic episodes of the Gold Rush. Manley survived and eventually reached California, and wrote this account of the experience forty-five years later.

Getting a Closer Look

Wanting to know as much as he could about the unexplored land back from the river, Powell took Bradley and climbed up a steep, ledgy wall in blistering sun. Somewhere on the cliff he made the mistake of jumping from one foothold to another, grabbing a projection of rock with his one hand. Then he found himself "rimmed," unable to go forward or back. Standing on tiptoe and clinging to the knob, he shouted to Bradley, above him, but Bradley could not reach him with his hand, and there was no halfway foothold to which he could descend. The cliff had neither brush nor pole; they had carried no rope with them.

Below his feet was a hundred-foot drop, a terrace, and then a longer drop. If he let himself go he might fall clear to the river's edge. By now his legs were trembling, his strength beginning to waver. As a desperation measure Bradley sat down on his ledge and yanked off his long drawers, which he lowered to Powell. With nice timing, Powell let got the knob, and half falling away from the cliff, grabbed the dangling underwear.

WALLACE STEGNER, known for his texts on American history, described Major John Powell's great interest in the unexplored reaches of the American Southwest in his book Beyond the Hundredth Meridian. *Major Powell often took barometric measurements of the depth of strata, heights of walls, fall of rivers, he also taught his crew members to use navigational instruments including the sextant. He constantly came down from the cliffs, exploring dangerously after dark, and stayed up nearly all nights making observations. And then, with an hour or two of sleep, would push off to run the river for awhile and tie up for more climbing, more observations.*

An Official Inspection Tour

So we rolled rapidly through summer and winter scenes, with sky of blue and air of amber purity, and when the round moon came up out from the snowy peaks, giving indescribable richness and softness to their whiteness, we kept on and on, now up mountain sides, now along the edge of precipices several hundred

feet high, down which the stumble of a horse or the error of a wheel would have plunged us; now crossing swollen streams, the water up to the coach doors, now stammering through morass and mire, plunging down and bounding up so that we passengers, instead of sleeping, were bruising heads and tangling legs and arms in enacting the tragedy of pop-corn over a hot fire and in a closed dish; and now from up among the clouds and snow, we tore down a narrow canyon at a breakneck rate, escaping a hundred over-turns and toppling on the river's brink until the head swam with dizzy apprehensions. Most picturesque of all the scenes of this day and night ride was the passage through Echo Canyon, a very miniature Rhine valley in all but vines and storied ruin. The only ruins in it were those of feeble fortifications which the Mormons set up when President Buchanan marched his army against them, but halted and went away without attack, leaving stores of provisions, wagons and ammunition, and a contempt for the government, neither of which the Mormons have quite exhausted yet. Early "sun-up" brought us to the last station, kept by a Mormon bishop with four wives, who gave us bitters and breakfast, the latter with green peas and strawberries, and then, leaving wife number one at his home, went on with us into the city for parochial visits to the other three, who are located at convenient distances around the Territory.

During the spring and summer of 1865, SAMUEL BOWLES accompanied Schuyler Colfax, Speaker of the United States House of Representatives, on a trip across the American territories. Bowles was one of the most ardent promoters of the west, and this enthusiasm was transformed into several books written in the 1860s. Soon after their return to the East, Bowles published his journal under the title Across the Continent; *it became so popular that subsequent editions were published in New York in 1866 and 1868.*

Discovering Fossils

Twelve miles from the Little Sandy, on descending a ravine, fossiliferous trunks of large trees, some of them nearly two feet in diameter, were observed upon the ground: the interior of some of these was hollowed out, but concentric rings were noticed near the circumference, and, in some specimens, longitudinal fibres were found in the interior. The bark appeared to be marked in places for the attachment of leaves of *Cycadeæ*, but they were all much weathered. The rocks on the river-bank were white compact sandstone, disposed in thin lamellæ, sandy and clayey shales, and a gray compact limestone, breaking with a conchoidal

Siltrock pillars in Bryce Canyon National Park. These formations, recalling church towers, are the result of natural weathering.

fracture. Some large portions of trunks of trees were protruding from the cliff, imbedded in apparently arenaceous shales. Some few specimens of fossils (*Nautilus and corals*) were collected, but, on account of the weathered state of the rocks, they were necessarily imperfect. The limestones contained but few fossils.

Thursday, August 9. – Our road to-day lay along the right bank of Big Sandy, until we reached Green River, which we crossed above the junction, and encamped a couple of miles below. The increased altitude, and the consequent dryness of the atmosphere, had so shrunk the woodwork of many of our wagon-wheels, that various expedients had to be resorted to, in order to prevent them from falling to pieces. To-day one of the wheels of the instrument-wagon, that precious and important portion of our train, became so weak from this cause that I was forced to take out nearly all the load, and distribute it among the other teams, to enable us to reach camp with it. We picked up a pair of wheels belonging to some emigrant-wagon, but they would not answer; so we were obliged to wedge up the wheel as well as we could, and to sink it in the river during the night, to swell the wood.

CAPTAIN HOWARD STANSBURY's survey of the Utah Territory, completed in 1850, marked a route to Utah from the settled areas of the American Mid-West, a route later followed by the Union Pacific Railway. The information in the journal proved to be of great value to later emigrants crossing the plains and mountains; as well, following its publication in London, England in 1852, served to encourage the flow of English Mormons to Utah.

"Roughing It"

In the morning, the tenth day out, we crossed Green River, a fine, large, limpid stream – stuck in it, with the water just up to the top of our mail-bed, and waited till extra teams were put on to haul us up the steep bank. But it was nice cool water, and besides it could not find any fresh place on us to wet.

At the Green River station we had breakfast – hot biscuits, fresh antelope steaks, and coffee – the only decent meal we tasted between the United States and Great Salt Lake City, and the only one we were ever really thankful for.

Think of the monotonous execrableness of the thirty that went before it, to leave this one simple breakfast looming up in my memory like a shot-tower after all these years have gone by!

The sculpture-like pillars in Bryce Canyon almost seem created by human hand. The Indians called them "red rocks standing in a bowl like humans".

At 5 P. M. we reached Fort Bridger, one hundred and seventeen miles from the South Pass, and one thousand and twenty-five miles from St. Joseph. Fifty- two miles further on, near the head of Echo Cañon, we met sixty United States soldiers from Camp Floyd. The day before, they had fired upon three hundred or four hundred Indians, whom they supposed gathered together for no good purpose. In the fight that had ensued, four Indians were captured, and the main body chased four miles, but nobody killed. This looked like business. We had a notion to get out and join the sixty soldiers, but upon reflecting that there were four hundred of the Indians, we concluded to go on and join the Indians.

Echo Cañon is twenty miles long. It was like a long, smooth, narrow street, with a gradual descending grade, and shut in by enormous perpendicular walls of coarse conglomerate, four hundred feet high in many places, and turreted like medieval castles. This was the most faultless piece of road in the mountains, and the driver said he would "let his team out." He did, and if the Pacific express-trains whiz through there now any faster than we did then in the stage-coach, I envy the passengers the exhilaration of it. We fairly seemed to pick up our wheels and fly – and the mail matter was

lifted up free from everything and held in solution! I am not given to exaggeration, and when I say a thing I mean it.

During 1861, SAMUEL CLEMENS accepted the position of Secretary to the Secretary of the Nevada Territory. While his intention was to visit the west for three months, he remained for over five years (during which time he began to sign himself as Mark Twain!). In his writings of the western years, Twain captured the essential spirit of the people, time, and place; the impressions, part narrative and part description, have not been equalled by any other writer of the period.

The "Devil's Gate"

Tuesday, July 31. – Ther. at sunrise, 40°. Leaving camp we continued up the valley of the Sweetwater, and passed the far-famed "Independence Rock," a large rounded mass of granite, which has frequently been described by travellers. It was covered with names of the passing emigrants, some of whom seemed determined, judging from the size of their inscriptions, that they would go down to posterity in all their fair proportions. A short distance beyond was a range of granite hills, stretching entirely across the valley, and

The awe-inspiring panorama of Bryce Canyon, seen from Peekaboo Trail.

continuous with a range extending to the north. Through this range the Sweetwater passes in a narrow cleft or gorge, about two hundred yards in length, called the "Devil's Gate". The space between the cliff, on either side, did not in some places exceed forty feet. The height was from three to four hundred feet, very nearly perpendicular, and, on the south side, overhanging. Through this romantic pass the river brawls and frets over broken masses of rock that obstruct its passage, affording one of the most lovely, cool, and refreshing retreats from the eternal sunshine without, that the imagination could desire. It is difficult to account for the river having forced its passage through the rocks at this point, as the hills, a very short distance to the south, are much lower, and, according to present appearance, present by no means such serious obstacles as had been here encountered. It is probable, that when the cañon was formed, stratified rocks obstructed it in that direction, and that these rocks have since disappeared by slow disintegration. The granite rocks of the pass were traversed in many places by dikes of trap, which were in some instances twenty feet thick, whose direction was east and west. South of the pass, at its eastern extremity, stratified rocks, consisting of conglomerate, were observed, in a nearly horizontal position, without exhibiting the least evidence of having been disturbed by the igneous rocks around which they were placed; indeed, they could be traced in close contact with the granite, without any displacement of the strata, proving that their formation must have been subsequent to that of the granite, from the disintegration of which they were composed. The conglomerate is of the same character as that which was observed before coming upon the carboniferous rocks. The rocks were not observed to have any marked dip. It is highly probable that they belong to a period subsequent to that in which the carboniferous rocks were formed, and that the eruption of granite took place after the latter formation, but before that of the conglomerate. No dikes of trap were observed in the granite, except in the immediate vicinity of the Devil's Gate.

After passing this remarkable cañon, we enter upon a broad level valley, bounded on each side by ranges of mountains, their summits broken into curious peaks and eminences entirely destitute of vegetation. Between these winds the Sweetwater, with a current more gentle than heretofore, its banks covered with grass. An accident occuring to one of the wagons, the remainder of the day was consumed in its repair. Thermometer at sunset, 70°.

Following on the heels of the Mormon emigration movement, and the increase in public interest in the *Utah Territory, CAPTAIN HOWARD STANSBURY of the Army Corps of Topographical Engineers began a systematic survey of the region in 1849; the results were published in 1852 by the United States Senate. Stansbury's dairy is a day-by-day account, with all the statistical information expected of a scientific report.*

The Overland Route

Monday, Oct. 1st. The country still continues mountainous and the road is the most rugged that we have yet met with and all pretty much down hill. Timber is somewhat scarce, and principally consists of cedar shrubberies and a dwarfish species of oak. Cactus fruit is abundant. Moving onward we descended a low ravine, skirted by sycamores and watered by a small stream; the grass, however, being indifferent. Here we halted to noon. In the afternoon we drove along the margin of the stream which is here bordered by a lofty mountain on either side, and massive rocks piled one above another to an immense height. In the course of the day we crossed this stream fifty-two times.

LORENZO D. ALDRICH wrote this journal entry in 1848. While Aldrich did not meet with success in his search for gold in California, he provided one of the earliest reports of the route from Fort Smith, Arkansas to San Diego, California, across the southern half of the Arizona Territory. The wagon train followed a trail that took them over difficult mountains and sandy deserts; Indians terrified them; rattlesnakes were a constant hazard; and quicksand in the rivers and sandstorms on the desert impeded them. However, it was malaria that killed Aldrich, contracted on a journey across the Isthmus of Panama on his return to New York from California.

Through Gray Canyon

The river played no favorites, and it showed no sign of conforming to their united wish for a letup. Beyond the Canyon of Desolation they ran directly into another, which they called Coal Canyon from the seams of lignite in the walls. It is now called Gray Canyon. And Gray Canyon was more of the same. In one bad rapid the river filled the channel from cliff to cliff, leaving not even the bare toehold of a portage. They had to let one boat down the full length of its line, then push off the second attached to it, and the third attached to the second, until all three were stretched out straining in the rapid, when the third was pulled in, then the second loosed and snubbed in, then the first. Then Bill Dunn, left on a rock in midstream, had to swim for it and be yanked in by those on shore.

Somewhat apart from Bryce Canyon is the more brilliantly coloured Red Canyon, whose sandstone formations are less worn by erosion than those of its geologically older neighbour.

37

Crushed by the massive glaciers of the ice age, these sand dunes in the eastern section of Zion National Park turned into rock.

It was bone-wrenching labor. Below that difficult lining job lay a portage, and below that a camp on a sandbeach in a hurricane of wind that blew all night and filled blankets, kettles, food, hair, eyes, ears, mouths, with sand. Desolation and Coal Canyons had been pretty continuous strain. Tempers were short, the rapids apparently endless. And then in a blink the unpredictable river gave them precisely what they craved: swift water, exhilarating little riffles and rapids that sped them along without labor and with a great lift of the spirit. They ran nineteen rapids in eighteen miles without the necessity of getting out of the boats, and at the end of Coal Canyon they burst out into open country again, a shimmering, blistered desert broken by circumeroded buttes of buff and gray and brown and slaty blue. Behind them, stretching in a long line east and west, were the Roan and Book Cliffs, cut to their base by the river's gorge, and meandering away in long wavy lines distorted by heat haze and the smoke of forest fires. To the northeast they saw snow mountains, the Uncompahgre Range in western Colorado. Across the valley the buttes lifted on the heat waves and hung dreamlike above the earth.

The river was deep, broad, quiet. Two hours below the mouth of Coal Canyon they found an Indian crossing where crude rafts were moored against the bank, and knew it for another of the very few practicable crossings in the canyon wilderness. At this point, now the site of Greenriver, Utah, where both Highway 50 and the Denver and Rio Grande cross, the old Spanish Trail, route of mule drivers between Taos and California, route of traveling mountain men and supply trains, found a way across the canyons.

WALLACE STEGNER is well-known for his historical works in the field of Americana. This account describes Major John Wesley Powell's 1869 voyage into the heart of the virtually unknown territory. The Powell Expedition, the first official journey of a white man through the one thousand mile route, was made in wooden boats and consisted of ten men. Incidently, Powell had lost an arm at the Battle of Shiloh.

The Stage to Lordsburg

They rode for an hour in this complete blackness, chilled and uncomfortable and half asleep, feeling the coach drag on a heavy-climbing grade. Gray dawn cracked through, followed by a sunless light rushing all across the flat desert now far below. The road looped from one barren shoulder to another and at sunup they

Heavily eroded sandstone pinnacles, like these in Capital Reef National Park, are typical features of the Colorado Plateau.

had reached the first bench and were slamming full speed along a boulder-strewn flat. The cattleman sat in the forward corner, the left corner of his mouth swollen and crushed, and when Henriette saw that her glance slid to Malpais Bill's knuckles. The army girl had her eyes closed, her shoulders pressing against the Englishman, who remained bolt upright with the sporting gun between his knees. Beside Henriette the gambler seemed to sleep, and on the middle bench Malpais Bill watched the land go by with a thin vigilance.

At ten they were rising again, with juniper and scrub pine showing on the slopes and the desert below them filling with the powdered haze of another hot day. By noon they reached the summit of the range and swung to follow its narrow rock-ribbed meadows. The gambler, long motionless, shifted his feet and caught the army girl's eyes.

"Shrieber's is directly ahead. We are past the worst of it."

ERNEST HAYCOX's Stage to Lordsburg *first appeared in April 1937; the story was turned into the John Ford film* Stagecoach *two years later. The film made both John Wayne and Monument Valley stars of the American Western.*

Quenching a Thirst

I witnessed, at the Pacific Springs, an instance of no little ingenuity on the part of some emigrant. Immediately alongside of the road was what purported to be a grave, prepared with more than usual care, having a headboard on which was painted the name and age of the deceased, the time of his death, and the part of the country from which he came. I afterward ascertained that this was only a ruse to conceal the fact that the grave, instead of containing the mortal remains of a human being, had been made a safe receptacle for divers casks of brandy, which the owner could carry no farther. He afterward sold his liquor to some traders farther on, who, by his description of its locality, found it without difficulty.

More than a collection of geographical data, the dairy of CAPTAIN HOWARD STANSBURY included comments on the Indians of the American Southwest, the emigrants already on the territories, the difficulties of travel and future prospects for development. In his 1849 report, Stansbury stated that the Mormon settlers seemed a happy and well-adjusted people, diligent in their vocations, and free from many of the faults that beset other people.

Impression of Arizona

We were out in Arizona, on the Painted Desert
    ground,
We had no place to call our home, and work could
    not be found.
Started to California, but our money it didn't last
    long,
I want to be in Oklahoma, be back in my old home.

Away out on the desert, where water is hard to find,
It's a hundred miles to Tempe and the wind blows
    all the time.
You will burn up in the daytime, yet you're cold
    when the sun goes down,
I want to be in Oklahoma, be back in my home
    town.

You people in Oklahoma, if you ever come West,
Have your pockets full of money, and you better be
    well dressed.
If you wind up on the desert, you're going to wish
    that you were dead,
You'll be longing for Oklahoma and your good old
    feather bed.

*"Arizona" was recorded from the singing of Jack Bryant
in Firebaugh, California, in 1940 as part of the United
States Library of Congress Archive of Folk Songs. The
writer of the song, presumably an Oklahoma native,
travelled through Arizona during the era of the dust
bowl and Depression. Tempe is thirty miles east of
Phoenix.*

A Descent to the River

The best thing to do was to descend to the bottom of the
Canyon; one must not only look at it but make contact
with it as well, and live in it for a whole day at least. At
the hotel we hired blue slacks, coats and gloves. The
mules were standing in a small enclosure, guarded by
two cowboys, whose clothes were a bit too showy;
they selected mounts suitable to our height and helped
us climb into the saddle. There were about a dozen of us
on this expedition. One of the cowboys took the head,
the other followed in rear. We were photographed in a
line at the top of the path: the photographs would await
us on our return. Below, a caravan of four mules laden
with hay went down the path cut in the rock. Then we
began to descend. A notice warned us on departure
that it was forbidden to bring dogs. The mules walked
with even paces; at each turning they lurched blindly
towards the precipice and swung back at the last

moment, quietly regaining the middle of the path: at
the end of an hour one was used to it. From time to time
a placard informed us of the geological age we had
reached; they pointed out, too, fossilised shells and
ferns. From top to bottom of the path telephone kiosks
had been planted and one could amuse oneself by
telephoning New York.

  We went down slowly, far slower than walking
pace. Little by little the scene changed, became more
real. We had left the cliff and were crossing a plateau
covered with thorny tufts, which from above had been
merely a coloured surface; now it had thickness and
smell, and each separate tuft existed, while the shades
of blue would vary. After three hours we stopped at the
edge of the flat rocks which fall to the river below: from
above it appeared as a thin, brilliant thread, but from
here it was a torrent with broad waters, swift-flowing,
tempting and dangerous; if I should bathe in them they
would change colour again. But we never got as far. We
halted higher up near some water. The mules ate hay
while we had our sandwiches and I dozed for a while
in the sun. No time to sleep, however: instead of this
expedition one would have liked to walk alone for a
long time along these paths, sleep at the water's edge,
and follow the river for nights on end on foot or by
canoe: to live in the intimacy of the Grand Canyon.
This intimacy must be difficult to achieve, for the
beauty of the place is at first too beautiful; no doubt its
more precious secrets are not easily learnt. But I envy
those to whom they have been revealed.

  *The French feminist, philosopher and novelist
SIMONE DE BEAUVOIR toured the United States in
1947, delivering lectures on the moral problems of the
post-war writer. Her impressions of the country were
published as* America Day by Day. *The book is crowded
with some shrewd observations on the American scene
and has been characterized as "a catalogue of the latest
anti-Americanisms abroad ... a handbook of popular
distortions and stale panaceas."*

New Senses – New Joys

We follow the stream of amber and bronze brawling
along its bed, with its frequent cascades and snow-
white foam. Through the cañon we fly – mountains not
only each side, but seemingly, till we get near right in
front of us – every rood a new view flashing, and each
flash defying description – on the almost perpendicular
sides, clinging pines, cedars, spruces, crimson sumach
bushes, spots of wild grass – but dominating all, those
towering rocks, rocks, rocks, bathed in delicate vari-
colors, with the clear sky of autumn overhead. New
senses, new joys, seem develop'd. Talk as you like, a

The Great White Throne in Zion National Park is well over 6,000 feet/2,000 metres high. The Mormons who settled here in the mid-nineteenth century gave this wildly romantic region of rocks and cliffs the name of the Mount of the Temple in Jerusalem: Zion.

typical Rocky Mountain cañon, or a limitless sea-like stretch of the great Kansas or Colorado plains, under favoring circumstances, tallies, perhaps expresses, certainly awakes, those grandest and subtlest element-emotions in the human soul, that all the marble temples and sculptures from Phidias to Thorwaldsen – all paintings, poems, reminiscences, or even music, probably never can.

WALT WHITMAN (1819–1892) was a key figure in the school of American Romanticism; his works have received critical recognition both in England and the United States. This selection is noted for its perception of man and nature, united and divine.

A Symphony of Color

Why, many a man has hardly noticed shapes in it at all. They are merely blobs of color. Color so rich and rampant that it floods the whole chasm; so powerful that it dissolves like acid all the shapes within it. Here, if you will, is a drama whose characters are colors: the royal purples, the angry reds, the mellow russets and monkish browns, soothing blues, shrieking yellows, tragic blacks and mystic whites, cool greens, pale lavenders and anemic grays.

A lifetime is too short to watch their infinite variations in key and tone. They change with every season, every hour, and with every change in light and weather.

In the blinding glare of a summer's noon its tints are so muted that the cañon seems a delicate pastel. But watch it at sunset. The yellows slowly deepen to orange; the salmon pinks to reds; the greens and blue-grays to damson blue; the lilacs to purple. Sunrise reverses the process. The whole chasm lifts bodily, inch by inch, toward light. The paint pot tips and spills over. The colors run and seep down the walls, collecting in pools below.

If it is a picture, winter frames it best. Preferably after a heavy snowfall when the plateaus are solid white, and better yet when every twig and needle is still sheathed in ice. Deeply inset in such a frame the cañon has all the warmth and color of a child's stereopticon slide held up to the table lamp. Into it snow never descends. A summer rainstorm is more potent. Then mists and clouds are formed below. Like tiny puffs from father's pipe they spurt out of the warm cañons and swelling like balloons gradually float to surface.

But the cold, clear, cloudless days of October – that is its time. Its colors stand out flat and positive. They relate

42

These petrified dunes in the eastern section of Zion National Park were formed 150 million years ago under the massive glaciers of the ice age.

it, not to the universal, but to the earth in which it is set. Red Supai sandstone, the rich red rock with the Indian name, the bright red Indian earth that stains land and river alike and give both their name. Green Tonto shale, green as pine and sage, bright as turquoise, clear as the turquoise sky above. Red and green on limestone white. These are its distinctive colors as they are the colors of the old Hopi ceremonial sashes, the masks of the giant Zuñi Shalako, the Navajo blankets, the fine old blankets of Chimayo so faded with their lost and unduplicated colors.

The author FRANK WATER spent much of his childhood in Navajo country, and travelled extensively in the mid-twentieth century in the American Southwest. His descriptive study of the beauty of the Grand Canyon is coupled with an understanding of the human character, and the relationship between nature and humanity.

Beyond the Blue Mesas

The canyon country does not always inspire love. To many it appears barren, hostile, repellent – a fearsome land of rock and heat, sand dunes and quicksand, cactus, thornbush, scorpion, rattlesnake, and agoraphobic distance. To those who see our land in that manner, the best reply is, yes, you are right, it is a dangerous and terrible place. Enter at your own risk. Carry water. Avoid the noonday sun. Try to ignore the vultures. Pray frequently.

For a few others the canyon country is worth only what they can dig out of it and haul away – to the mills, to the power plants, to the bank.

For more and more of those who now live here, however, the great plateau and its canyon wilderness is a treasure best enjoyed through the body and spirit, in situ as the archeologists say, not through commercial plunder. It is a regional, four separate mountain ranges nicely distributed about the region, and more hills, holes, humps and hollows, reefs, folds, salt domes, swells and grabens, buttes, benches and mesas, synclines, monoclines, and anticlines than you can ever hope to see and explore in one lifetime, and you begin to arrive at an approximate picture of the plateau's surface appearance.

An approximate beginning. A picture framed by sky and time in the world of natural appearances. Despite the best efforts of a small army of writers, painters, photographers, scientists, explorers, Indians, cowboys, and wilderness guides, the landscape of the Colorado

Rainbow Bridge, a mere five minutes by foot from the wharf on Lake Powell, Utah.

Rainbow Bridge is one of the mightiest natural wonders of the Colorado Plateau The Indians venerated this spectacular stone bridge as a petrified rainbow. Not until 1909 did they alert the whites to its existence.

Plateau lies still beyond the reach of reasonable words. Or unreasonable representation. This is a landscape that has to be seen to be believed, and even then, confronted directly by the senses, it strains credulity.

Comprehensible, yes. Perhaps nowhere is the basic structure of the earth's surface so clearly, because so nakedly, revealed. And yet – when all we know about it is said and measured and tabulated, there remains something in the soul of the place, the spirit of the whole, that cannot be fully assimilated by the human imagination.

EDWARD ABBEY, a modern American writer, is also an active conservationist. His portrait of Canyon Country, which appeared in print in 1977, celebrates the splendour of nature while also giving a warning about the growing threat posed by human ignorance and carelessness.

On Snow Peak

Here, on the summit, where the sillness was absolute, unbroken by any sound, and the solitude complete, we thought ourselves beyond the region of animated life; but while we were sitting on the rock, a solitary bee (*Bombus*, the humblebee) came winging his flight from the eastern valley, and lit on the knee of one of the men.

It was a strange place, the icy rock and the highest peak of the Rocky Mountains, for a lover of warm sunshine and flowers; and we pleased ourselves with the idea that he was the first of his species to cross the mountain barrier – a solitary pioneer to foretell the advance of civilization. I believe that a moment's thought would have made us let him continue his way unharmed; but we carried out the law of this country, where all animated nature seems at war, and, seizing him immediately, put him in at least a fit place – in the leaves of a large book, among the flowers we had collected on our way. The barometer stood at 18.293, the attached thermometer at 44°; giving for the elevation of this summit thirteen thousand five hundred and seventy feet above the Gulf of Mexico, which may be called the highest flight of the bee. It is certainly the highest known flight of that insect.

JOHN CHARLES FREEMONT (1813–1890) was the last of the great explorers of the interior of North America, a man who made the unknown countries known. He first crossed the Rocky Mountains in 1842 with Kit Carson as guide. Freemont was appointed governor of Arizona Territory in 1878.

Slickrock Canyons are hard to find and only manageable by experienced mountain climbers. The most famous of them, pictured here, is Antelope Canyon in Arizona, whose walls were "sculpted" by silty water.

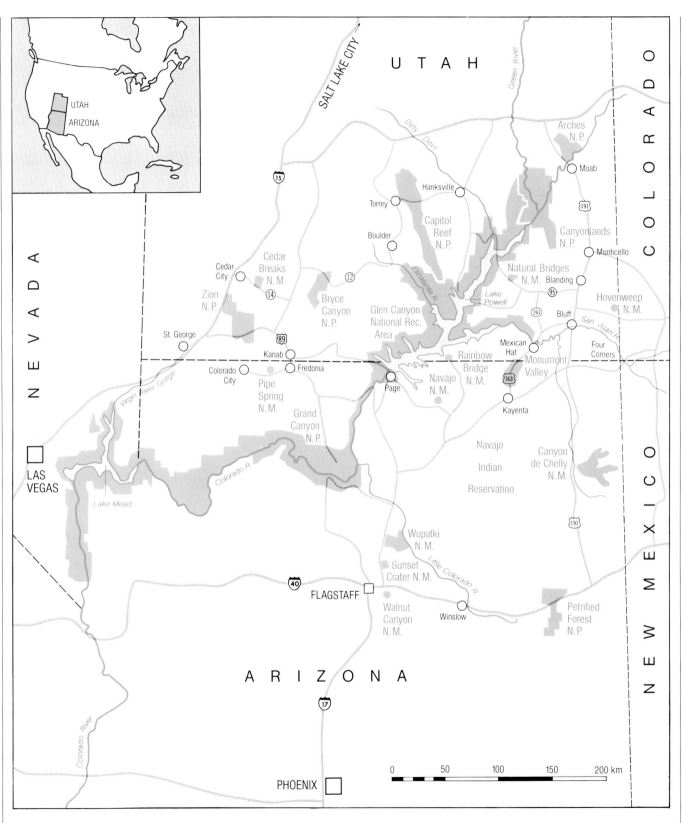

Italicized numbers refer to colour photographs.

GENERAL INFORMATION

ARIZONA. Mountain state in the American Southwest, bordering on New Mexico, California, Utah and Mexico. Its land area of 114,000 square miles/ 295,000 square kilometres makes it larger than Great Britain. Its population is expanding rapidly as Arizona lies in the attractive American "Sun Belt". Two-fifths of Arizona's land area is part of the → Colorado Plateau in the northwest with its famous national parks, → Grand Canyon and → Petrified Forest. Other tourist attractions include the cactus forests in Saguaro National Monument near Tucson and Organ Pipe Cactus National Monument on the southern border with Mexico. Arizona largely has an arid or semiarid climate, i.e. it is hot in summer and, apart from occasional thunderstorms, generally dry, with more than 200 cloudless days per year.

UTAH. Mountain state in the western part of the United States, lying between Colorado, Arizona, Nevada, Idaho and Wyoming (at Four Corners it also touches New Mexico). Its land area of 85,000 square miles/220,000 square kilometres makes it almost as large as Great Britain. The state capital, Salt Lake City, was founded in 1847 by the Mormon patriarch Brigham Young. Geographically, more than half of Utah belongs to the → Colorado Plateau, the western third to the Great Basin, and the rest to the Rocky Mountains. Apart from the Great Salt Lake in the Great Basin, Utah's most famous points of interest all lie on the Colorado Plateau: → Arches, → Bryce Canyon, → Canyonlands, → Capitol Reef, → Zion National Park and many other nature reserves. Except in its southwest section, which has almost subtropical conditions, Utah is a desert state: its summers are hot with frequent thunderstorms, its winters cold and dry. Due to its dry winter climate Utah can boast of the "greatest snow on earth": its marvelous powder snow.

WEATHER CONDITIONS

The best time to visit Arizona and Utah is from late August to mid October. In July and August it is very hot: over 115° Fahrenheit/45° Celsius and there are frequent thunderstorms, especially in Utah. Thunderstorms are rare in September and October, and the skies are usually clear. Even if daytime temperatures go above 90° Fahrenheit/30° Celsius it becomes cool at night. At higher altitudes (e.g. → Bryce Canyon at 7,500 feet/ 2,400 metres) it can become bitingly cold at night, and even go below freezing.
As an alternative we recommend the months of May and June, particularly for parks such as → Capitol Reef and → Zion which have interesting vegetation.

POINTS OF INTEREST

ANTELOPE CANYON, Arizona. This is the most famous of the little-known → Slick-

rock Canyons. About five miles/eight kilometres long, it leads in three stages, etched in sandstone, to → Lake Powell. Between these stages the creator of this canyon, Antelope Creek, sometimes flows on open ground after a rainstorm. The middle stage is only about 500 feet/ 150 metres long and ends directly beneath a bridge on Highway 98 running from Page to Kaibito. Here, about ten minutes from Page and just before the Navajo Power Plant, you can

Rock paintings by the Anasazi.

simply walk into the canyon. To reach the upper section, called Corkscrew Canyon, you have to walk about two miles/three kilometres, though a dirt

track allows you to drive halfway. The lower section begins a mere 600 yards/ 500 metres from the end of the middle stage. The visible cleft seems far too narrow, but it is possible to squeeze through, and a system of ropes and ladders helps you over the first steps. The canyon is situated on the → Navajo Indian Reservation extending to Lake Powell. To enter the canyon grounds you need permission from the Navajo authorities. A permit can be obtained for

Arches National Park.

a few dollars at the LeChee Chapter House near → Page, tel. (602) 698-3273 (ask for directions). *47*

ARCHES NATIONAL PARK, Utah. This park, located about ten minutes by car from → Moab, is one of the smaller parks on the → Colorado Plateau. It takes up 115 square miles/297 square kilometres and has an altitude of 4,000 to 5,500 feet/ 1,200 to 1,800 metres. Its 90 stone arches, spanning from 3 to 275 feet/1 to 89 metres, make it the world's most impressive collection of this natural wonder. The widest of these, Landscape Arch (275 feet), is already so slender that it is in danger of collapsing. The freestanding Delicate Arch is considered the most beautiful of its kind on earth. It can be reached easily in about half an hour by foot from the nearest parking lot. The park has an asphalt road leading to the Garden of Eden, Windows Section and Devils Garden. *6/7, 9, 10, 11*

BRYCE CANYON NATIONAL PARK, Utah (55 square miles/145 square kilometres, 7,500 to 8,500 feet/2,400 to 2,750 metres altitude), is not a canyon but a gathering of red and white stone pillars (→ hoodoos) in a gigantic amphitheatre. The Paiute Indians gave this spot the name Unka-timpewa-wince-pockich (red rocks standing in a bowl like humans). Its present name derives from a Mormon couple named Bryce who tried to settle here. They, too, left behind

Above: Canyon de Chelly. Below: Canyonlands National Park.

a fitting description: "a hell of a place to lose a cow". Today Bryce Canyon is seen for what it is: a wonder of nature without equal. *31, 33, 34/35*

BURR TRAIL. Though lacking a blacktop and very rough in parts, this dirt road can be managed by a normal automobile, except after heavy rainfall. It runs between Boulder and Torrey, Utah, along → Capitol Reef National Park through a lonely but majestic landscape – the → Colorado Plateau at its best.

CAINEVILLE BADLANDS, Utah. This is the unofficial name of the especially bleak and bizarre badlands lying between → Capitol Reef National Park and Hanksville, Utah. Heavily eroded blue-grey and reddish mountains. The term "badlands" refers to non-arable country-side. Most of the reserves on the → Colorado Plateau are badlands.

CANYON DE CHELLY NATIONAL MONUMENT, Arizona, three interlinked gorges over 900 feet/300 metres deep, on the → Navajo Indian Reservation near Chinle. The floor of the canyon is cultivated by the Navajo during the summer. Its north and south rims can be reached by car. There are many wonderful scenic lookouts into this calm and peaceful canyon, which also has a large number of abandoned pre-Columbian cliff dwellings and beautiful patterns of desert varnish.

At the end of the road along the southern rim of the canyon is Spider Rock, a freestanding red sandstone pinnacle 760 feet/245 metres high. This geological formation, as tall as the Empire State Building, must be one of nature's mightiest wonders. The valley floor is closed to automobiles, but a well-organized Navajo tour by cross-country vehicle should not be missed. You will also be told much about the history of the → Navajos and the canyon. *17, 21*

CANYONLANDS NATIONAL PARK, Utah (525 square miles/1,366 square kilometres, 3,700 to 5,900 feet/1,200 to 1,900 metres altitude). Not until 1964 did this gigantic rocky desert attain the status of a national park. It is still virtually inaccessible. It is divided into three parts by the → Colorado and Green Rivers, which converge inside the park at Confluence. Each of these parts – Sky, Needles and Maze – is reachable only "from the outside". The easiest to reach is the northeast section, Island in the Sky. A blacktopped track leads from the Moab-Green River road to Grand View Point and Green River Overlook, with rivetting views of Monument Basin, Green River and the → Colorado (formerly Grand River). Branch 211 of Highway 191 between Moab and Monticello is a blacktopped track leading into the Needles District to the base of Elephant Hill. From there you can only proceed further by foot or jeep. One special highlight in the Needles District is Angel Arch. The most remote and isolated section is the Maze District, which can be reached by driving along Highway 24 between Hanksville and Green River to the Han's Flat ranger station. Once again, from there you will have to go by foot or cross-country vehicle (difficult). *2*

CAPITOL REEF NATIONAL PARK, Utah (376 square miles/979 square kilometres, 5,000 to 8,000 feet/1,600 to 2,600 metres altitude). This park has the advantage of lying apart from larger towns and is therefore visited less frequently than the others. Its rock structures are particularly interesting. A round-trip tour leads to many natural attractions. Especially impressive is Capitol Gorge at the end of Scenic Drive, a dirt track leading through a claustrophobically narrow canyon. *39*

CEDAR BREAKS NATIONAL MONUMENT, Utah. A steep-banked amphitheatre with → siltrock pillars similar to those in → Bryce Canyon. The upper rim has an altitude of over 9,000 feet/3,000 metres, making it higher than the plateau of Bryce Canyon. A 45-minute drive from Cedar City on Highway *14, 32*

COLORADO PLATEAU. This vast area, about as large as the newly reunited state of Germany, covers the southern half of Utah and the northern half of Arizona as well as parts of Colorado and New Mexico. Actually it is not a plateau, as its name suggests, but rather a flat basin with an average altitude of 4,600 feet/1,500 metres above sea level. In the course of time it was rent and disfigured by volcanic uplifts and furrowed by the canyons of its rivers, including the Colorado, Green, Escalante and San Juan.
Throughout the Colorado Plateau, and especially in its national parks, national monuments and state parks, there reigns a variety of topography staggering the imagination. Mesas and canyons, natural bridges and arches, cliffs and needles, pillars and domes, towers and pinnacles, all in variegated colours (predominantly red), pass by in endless review. Its geographical centre is Kayenta, Arizona, but for visiting purposes the hub of the Colorado Plateau is → Moab, Utah.

COLORADO RIVER. Originating at a height of nearly 10,000 feet/3,000 metres in the Colorado Rockies in Rocky Mountains National Park, the Colorado flows 1,500 miles/2,335 kilometres to the Gulf of California. Together with its tributaries, it drains an area of 243,000 square miles/632,000 square kilometres, roughly twice the size of Great Britain. It has been called the most intensively used river on earth and is so heavily exploited for irrigating the deserts of Utah, California and Arizona that only a tiny saline trickle reaches the Gulf. Before the Hoover and Glen Canyon dams were built the Colorado was, in certain spots and seasons, a wild and unruly monster that could reach speeds of 12.5 mph/

Dead Horse Point State Park.

Coral Pink Sand Dunes.

20 km/h (today its average speed is 2.25 mph/7 km/h) and a volume of over 2 million gallons/8,500,000 litres per second! On 13 September 1927 alone it swept away a record 27 million tons of mud in a mere 24 hours. On an average, the Colorado used to transport 390,000 tons of silt per day, the equivalent of 40,000 ten-ton trucks. Today, four-fifths of all the sediment transported by the Colorado comes to rest in Lake Powell – an average of 320,000 tons per day! This sedimentation has given → Lake Powell a new purpose in addition to the generation of hydroelectric power: namely, to prolong the life of Lake Mead, which now only receives one-fifth of the earlier amount of silt. Lake Powell, on the other hand, will silt up in 700 to 1,000 years. Trips by boat and raft through the → Grand Canyon of the Colorado are very popular and are booked at least one year in advance. They start at Lee's Ferry and end, 270 miles/450 kilometres later, in Lake Mead. *2*

CORAL PINK SAND DUNES STATE RESERVE, Utah. Following the signposted turnoff from Highway 89 between Kanab and Rockville one immediately comes to a large area of pastel pink or, predominantly, yellowish sand dunes.
This attractive park, with its interesting desert vegetation, is unfortunately marred by the presence of off-road vehicles, especially three-wheeled motorcycles with special tyres, which are gradually destroying the shapes of the dunes.

The Grand Canyon.

DEAD HORSE POINT STATE PARK, Utah. This park, located about 30 miles/ 50 kilometres north of Moab, is reached via a blacktopped road. It offers a splendid view of the → Colorado and the stony wilderness of → Canyonlands National Park. Many visitors even find this view more impressive than that of the → Grand Canyon. There are several theories to explain the origin of the park's name. The most credible is that this ledge, surrounded by perpendicular cliffs and connected to the tablelands by a single narrow path, once served as a corral and that the horses kept there died of thirst after being abandoned.

EL CAPITAN, Utah. This volcanic cone near Kayenta is the sacred mountain of the → Navajo, who refer to it as the centre of the universe.

FISHER TOWERS, Utah. A spot of especially bizarre rock towers, some of them seemingly as thin as paper. It is located about 25 miles/40 kilometres east of Moab. *27*

FLAGSTAFF, Arizona. Founded in 1880, this town of 35,000 is the largest on the → Colorado Plateau. It is conveniently situated for excursions to the → Grand Canyon, → Meteor Crater, → Petrified Forest, → Sunset Crater and → Wupatki National Park and National Monument. The local industries are forestry and animal husbandry.

GLEN CANYON NATIONAL RECREATION AREA, Arizona and Utah. This area includes → Lake Powell and its adjoining shorelines. It borders on → Grand Canyon National Park in the southwest, → Capitol Reef and → Canyonlands National Park in the north, and the → Navajo Indian Reservation in the southeast.

GOBLIN VALLEY STATE RESERVE, Utah. Located north of Hanksville at the end of a good-quality gravel road, this park is a collection of hundred of "goblins" in soft red sandstone (→ siltrock), some of them extremely bizarre. It was only discovered in 1949 by a Mr. Chaffin, who called the spot Mushroom Valley, and has been a state park since 1964.

GOULDING'S TRADING POST, Utah. Established by Mr. Goulding in 1920 for trade with the → Navajo, this comfortable motel is the closest to → Monument Valley about 6 miles/10 kilometres away. Its guided tours of the valley are highly recommended.

GRAND CANYON NATIONAL PARK, Arizona. This canyon, probably created by the → Colorado and its tributaries, is neither the longest nor the deepest on earth. But it is doubtlessly the most impressive and easily the most popular. The Canyon of the "Grand" (as the Colorado River used to be known) became a national park in 1919. Since then the park has been enlarged several times, and now covers 1,900 square miles/4,930 square kilometres; it is the second largest national park after Yellowstone. Grand Canyon National Park is divided by the Colorado into the North and South Rims. At the scenic lookout at Bright Angel, the North Rim is about 1,000 feet/360 metres higher than the lookouts on the other side. From the North Rim, the plateau lies about one mile/1,750 metres above the Colorado

Muley Point.

River, while the park itself, measured along the river, is 720 miles/450 kilometres long. The layers of rock exposed to view range in age from relatively recent to about two billion years old. Traces of these organisms, however, have yet to be discovered in the Grand Canyon. *22/23*

HOVENWEEP NATIONAL MONUMENT, Utah. Ruins of → Anasazi pueblos with defensive towers and irrigation systems, located near Blanding and Bluff, Utah.

HUNT'S MESA. A little-known scenic lookout with a unique view of → Monument Valley, reachable only by one of the most difficult jeep tours on the → Colorado Plateau. The tours start at Kayenta, Arizona; the path must be located with the help of a guide. *4/5*

KODACHROME BASIN STATE RESERVE, Utah. A group of "chimney rocks", colourful → siltrock towers located south of Bryce Canyon and reachable via a gravel road.

LAKE POWELL. A reservoir created by a dam on the Colorado River and lying 95 percent in Utah and 5 percent in Arizona. Its waters flooded the obscure → Glen Canyon, "the place no one knew". Construction of the 670-foot/216-metre dam lasted from 1956 to 1963, and it took 17 years for the reservoir to reach its final height of 3,800 feet/1,230 metres above sea level. It generates 960 megawatts of hydroelectric power. On satellite photographs the lake, with its 96 lateral canyons, looks like a many-pronged bluish lightning bolt. Its shoreline of nearly 2,000 miles/3,140 kilometres is twice as long as the West Coast of America without Alaska. At its longest point the lake reaches 190 miles/330 kilometres; it contains 43 billion cubic yards/33 million cubic metres of water with a total surface area of 255 square miles/660 square kilometres, making it one of the largest reservoirs in the world. Besides its actual purpose – to regulate the Colorado and generate hydroelectric power – Lake Powell is also a favourite recreation area for motorboats and houseboats of all sizes. *44/45*

METEOR CRATER, Arizona. Located near Winslow about 50 miles/80 kilometres southeast of → Flagstaff, this crater (formerly known as Diablo Canyon) is one of the largest and best preserved of its kind. Here, about 22,000 years ago, a 60,000-ton meteor struck the earth with a velocity of nearly 30,000 miles/45,000 kilometres per hour, releasing the same amount of energy as several hydrogen bombs. An estimated 500 million tons of rock and debris were catapulted into the atmosphere. The crater has a diameter of nearly 4,000 feet/1,265 metres and is about 550 feet/175 metres deep.

MEXICAN HAT, Utah. A → Navajo settlement in the vicinity of → Monument Valley and → Goosenecks State Reserve. It takes its name from a sandstone tower topped by a hat-like stone table.

MOAB, Utah. This town is the tourist hub of the → Colorado Plateau. From 10 to 40 minutes from Moab by car are the entrances to → Arches National Park, → Dead Horse Point State Park and → Canyonlands National Park (Islands in the Sky section), as well as Castle Valley, the → Fisher Towers and Nine Mile Canyon. Moab is also a starting point for peaceful journeys by raft on the → Colorado.

MONUMENT VALLEY, Navajo Tribal Park. This is part of the → Navajo Indian Reservation, located jointly in Utah and Arizona about 25 miles/40 kilometres southwest of → Mexican Hat, Utah, or 25 miles north of Kayenta, Arizona. Monument Valley is famous throughout

The Petrified Forest.

the world as the scene of many Western movies. For those travelling by private car it can be reached by a dirt track in a roundtrip journey of about 18 miles/28 kilometres. Another dirt track of about the same length can only be travelled by guides and cross-country vehicles. Hiking is prohibited. At any time of the day Monument Valley conveys an impression of sublime grandeur which can reach an awe-inspiring solemnity at sunrise and, especially, at sunset. *4/5, 13, 14, 15, 18/19*

MULEY POINT, Utah. Scenic lookout over the → Goosenecks of the San Juan River and → Monument Valley. Little can be seen of the river itself. Gravel road from Highway 261 north of → Mexican Hat.

NATURAL BRIDGES NATIONAL MONU-MENT, Utah. Located north of → Mexican Hat on Highway 95 are three natural bridges of white sandstone, the largest

over 200 feet/80 metres high with a span of 250 feet/66 metres. There are also many ruins of the → Anasazi.

NAVAJO INDIAN RESERVATION. Territory assigned to the → Navajo and → Hopi tribes consisting of nearly 25,000 square miles/65,000 square kilometres. Located in the states of → Arizona, New Mexico and → Utah, it is semi-autonomous with its own police force and judicial system. Its administrative centre, and the seat of its tribal council, is Window Rock, Arizona.

NAVAJO NATIONAL MONUMENT, Arizona. Three former Navajo Indian settlements – Betatakin, Keet Seel and Inscription House – located about 20 miles/30 kilometres west of Kayenta. The last-named settlement is reachable on a half-day tour by climbing up more than 700 steps!

OLD PARIAH GHOST TOWN, Utah. This ghost town, located at the end of a northern turnoff from Highway 89 from Page to Kanab, was rebuilt for a movie. It has a few woodframe houses standing before clay hills with layers of brown, white, green and red cinnabar. Seldom visited today. Caution: The normally reliable approach road can be transformed by rain into a slippery quagmire.

PARIAH WILDERNESS TRAILHEAD, Utah. South of Highway 89 from Page to Kanab

begins the Pariah Wilderness Trail, a challenging and, during thunderstorms, perilous hike to Lee's Ferry at the northern end of → Grand Canyon National Park. The trailhead is marked by curious formations in pinkish white sandstone.

PETRIFIED FOREST NATIONAL PARK, Arizona. (146 square miles/380 square kilometres, 5,000 to 6,000 feet/1,600 to 1,900 metres altitude). This park, which is part of the Painted Desert, is different from the other national parks on the → Colorado Plateau. It consists of red, light grey, green and blue hills of clay and loam containing most of the petrified tree trunks famous the world over. These trees, many of which have been preserved intact, are about 200 million years old. After falling in primeval swamps they were covered by mud, and, in the course of time, their organic matter was replaced by silicic acid, which caused tiny quartz crystals to form in the cells of the wood.

PIPE SPRING NATIONAL MONUMENT, Arizona. Formerly a fortified Mormon settlement, located about 25 miles/ 40 kilometres from Kaibab.

RAINBOW BRIDGE NATIONAL MONU-MENT, Utah. Venerated by the Indians as a petrified rainbow, this natural bridge was not "discovered" by white men until 1909. Formerly reachable only on long and exhausting trails, it is now easily accessible by round-trip boat tours departing twice a day from → Wahweap Marina. The 50-mile/80-kilometre tour from the marina to Rainbow Bridge is managed in two hours. Anyone who has seen Rainbow Bridge, with its span of 260 feet/84 metres and height of 275/ 88 metres, will agree that this perfectly formed structure is the greatest of all the natural wonders on the → Colorado Plateau. *44/45, 46*

RED CANYON, Utah. Located in Dixie National Forest, this forerunner of Bryce Canyon has → hoodoos which are even more brilliantly coloured than those of its more famous neighbour but are generally ignored by tourists. *37*

SHAFER TRAIL. Formerly an Indian footpath, this trail leads from the mining town of Potash near → Moab to the higher plain of → Canyonlands National Park. It was turned into a jeep track by uranium prospectors. The section between the entrance to Canyonlands National Park and the turnoff to → White Rim Trial can also be travelled by automobile. This is the quickest route from Moab to the entrance of Canyonlands National Park (Island of the Sky section), and leads through impressive scenery with views of the → Colorado, Walking Rocks and dark red sandstone cliffs.

SLICKROCK CANYONS. For the most part a very narrow sandstone gorge whose walls have been polished into fantastic shapes by the sandy water. Though recently opened to the public, Slickrock Canyons are difficult to find and enter. *47*

SUNSET CRATER NATIONAL MONUMENT, Arizona. Volcanic ash cone in the San Francisco Peaks north of → Flagstaff, dating from the eleventh century. It may be taken in on the way to → Grand Canyon, but can also be skipped.

TOROWEAP OVERLOOK, Arizona. A scenic viewpoint near Tuweep that looks out over the → Colorado River and ancient lava flows. It is seldom visited, being reachable only from Fredonia, Arizona, or Colorado City, Utah, over nearly 65 miles/100 kilometres of gravel roads. On several occasions the lava flows blocked the course of the Colorado, forming walls up to 500 feet/160 metres high and damming the river for 480 miles/300 kilometres. Overlook also offers a view of Lava Falls, the most impressive whitewater rapids in the → Grand Canyon.

VIRGIN RIVER GORGE, Utah. On the route from Salt Lake City to Cedar City and Las Vegas, Interstate 15 crosses the canyon of the Virgin River, where it descends from the → Colorado Plateau into the Great Basin. Even though Interstate 15 is a four-lane freeway, the drive through this gorge is breathtaking and a masterpiece of road construction. The Virgin River flows into Lake Mead, another reservoir of the → Colorado River.

WAHWEAP MARINA, Arizona. Located a few miles west of Page, this marina is the largest yachting harbour on → Lake Powell, the others being Dangling Rope, Bullfrog, Hite and Halls Crossing. It boasts a large hotel and moorings for hundreds of motorboats and houseboats, which can be taken out on hire. Wahweap is an Indian name meaning "bitter water".

WALNUT CANYON NATIONAL MONUMENT, Arizona. Indian ruins beneath overhanging cliffs, located east of

Musselman Arch, White Rim Trail.

→ Flagstaff and dating from the twelfth and thirteenth centuries.

WHITE RIM TRAIL. A jeep trail through magnificent scenery along White Rim in the Island in the Sky section of → Canyonlands National Park. Even experienced drivers cannot manage the 110-mile/180-kilometre roundtrip from Moab in a single day. There are no sources of water along the entire trail! From the point where White Rim Trail branches off from Shafer Trail you can travel about 4 miles/7 kilometres by car to Musselman Arch, which is over 90 feet/30 metres long and almost 10 feet/3 metres wide. Being smooth on the top, this is the only arch on the entire → Colorado Plateau that can be crossed.

WUPATKI NATIONAL MONUMENT, Arizona. Remains of an Indian settlement located north of → Flagstaff and dating from the pre-Columbian era (twelfth and thirteenth centuries), including multi-storey buildings. Condi-

tions for settlement were favoured by the fertile ash spewed out by the nearby → Sunset Crater volcano.

YE-BE-CHAI. Together with Totem Pole, this stone tower is one of the most striking of its kind in → Monument Valley. Its name is Navajo for "dancing gods".

ZION NATIONAL PARK, Utah (225 square miles/590 square kilometres, 4,000 to 8,000 feet/1,200 to 2,600 metres altitude). Compared to other national parks on the → Colorado Plateau, Zion is refreshingly green, being watered by the → Virgin River. Delightful hikes can be taken from the floor of the canyon, for example to Emerald Pools. On this path you can pass beneath several small waterfalls. Weeping Rock is another interesting sight, reachable even by wheelchair. The water constantly seeping out here has spent many years underway from the surrounding plateau. Another hike leads us from the north end of the canyon to the Narrows, a deep gorge through which passes the Virgin River. In place this gorge is so narrow that one has to wade through the river or, during high water, even swim through it! The eastern section of the park is completely different in character. Here, more than 4,500 feet/1,500 metres above sea level, we find petrified sand dunes in grotesque shapes and forms. *38, 41, 42, 43*

BRIEF GLOSSARY

ANASAZI ("they who went away"). Navajo term for the early native inhabitants of the → Colorado Plateau. There is no unbroken tradition connecting the Anasazi and the present-day tribes of the → Navajo, → Hopi, Paiute and Havasupai. Hence, the rock inscriptions they left behind (at Petroglyphs or Newspaper Rocks) have never been deciphered. Nor is it known why the Anasazi abandoned their pueblos (cliff dwellings) in such apparent haste, or why they built them in this almost inaccessible area in the first place.

DESERT VARNISH. The porous sandstone of the → Colorado Plateau is rich in iron and manganese, giving it a generally red, reddish-brown or brown hue. When water seeps into this stone it dissolves the iron- and manganese-rich minerals and carries them to the lower surfaces. Here the water evaporates and the minerals (oxides and hydroxides of iron and manganese) remain to form an enamel-like crust. Especially striking deposits of desert varnish can be seen from Antelope House in → Canyon de Chelly and in → Capitol Reef National Park. *21*

GOOSENECKS. An American term for sharp serpentine bends in a river bed. A good example are the goosenecks in the San Juan River near → Mexican Hat, Utah, where the river makes three 180-degree turns in rapid succession. An excellent view can be had from Goosenecks State Reserve, a natural platform nearly 1,000 feet/305 metres above the deeply etched bends located at the end of Road 316, a four-mile/seven-kilometre turnoff from Highway 261. Surprisingly this natural wonder, probably the only one of its kind on earth, is seldom visited. *28/29*

HOODOO. According to Webster's Collegiate Dictionary, a hoodoo is "something that brings bad luck". But to the Bryce Canyon Newspaper it is "a pinnacle, pillar or odd shaped rock left standing by the forces of erosion". *34/35*

HOPI. Today the "Hopitah", or "people of peace", live on the arid tablelands of Black Mesa in the northeast section of → Arizona. This tribe of native Americans has about 10,000 members living in clans. They are famous for their sacred kachina dances, which tourists are only allowed to visit if personally invited by a Hopi.

NAVAJO. Name given by the "whites" to a tribe of native Americans (their own name is "Dinneh" meaning the people). They migrated here from Canada around the year 1400. Following the "conquest" of North America they suffered a tragic

Hoodoos.

fate of displacement and massacre. Today the Navajo, with their 150,000 members, are the largest of Indian tribes, and live primarily in the vicinity of Four Corners.

SILTROCK. In addition to the term → slickrock, geologists also speak of siltrock. This refers to those many formations on the → Colorado Plateau that seem, at least to laymen, to be made of dried mud. Among these formations are the pillars and towers (→ hoodoos) of → Bryce Canyon, → Goblin Valley, → Red Canyon and → Cedar Breaks.

SLICKROCK. This term refers to rock formations, normally of sandstone, which have been polished by wind or water. Many striking phenomena on the → Colorado Plateau are made of slickrock: → arches, bridges, canyon walls. Slickrock on a smaller scale can be found in → Slickrock Canyons.

LIST OF SOURCES AND ILLUSTRATIONS

Edward Abbey, *The Journey Home*. New York: E.P. Dutton, 1977. Copyright © 1977 by Edward Abbey. Used by permission of the publisher, Dutton, an imprint of New American Library, a division of Penguin Books USA Inc.
Lorenzo D. Aldrich, *A Journal of the Overland Route to California*. Lansingburgh: Kirkpatrick Printers, 1851.
Samuel Bowles, *Across the Continent*. New York: Hurd & Houghton, 1865.
Malcolm Cowley (ed.), *The Complete Poetry and Prose of Walt Whitman in Two Volumes*. Volume II. New York: Pellegrini & Cudahy, 1948.
Simone de Beauvoir, *America Day by Day*. Trans. Patrick Dudley. London: Gerald Duckworth & Co. Ltd., 1952. (*L'Amerique au Jour le Jour*. Paris: Editions Paul Morihien, 1950).
Duncan Emrich (comp.), *American Folk Poetry. An Anthology*. Boston: Little, Brown, and Company, 1974.
John Charles Freemont, *Report on the Exploration of the Country Lying between the Missouri River and the Rocky Mountains*. New York, 1843.
Ernest Haycox, "Stage to Lordsburgh", in *Stagecoach. A Film by John Ford and Dudley Nichols*. New York: Simon and Schuster, 1971.
William Lewis Manley, *Death Valley in '49*. San José: Pacific Tree and Vine Co., 1894.
Washington Matthews, *Navaho Legends*. Boston: Houghton, Mifflin, and Company, 1897.
Narrative of the Adventures of Zenas Leonard. Clearfield: D.W. Moore, 1839.
Howard Stansbury, *An Expedition to the Valley of the Great Salt Lake of Utah*. London: Sampson, Low, Son, and Co., 1852.
Wallace Stegner, *Beyond the Hundredth Meridian*. Boston: Houghton, Mifflin Co., 1954.
Mark Twain, *Roughing It*. London: Harper & Row, 1913.
Frank Water, *The Colorado*. New York: Rinehart & Co., Inc. 1946.

We would like to thank all copyright holders and publishers for their kind permission to reprint. Despite intensive efforts on our part, we were not able to contact all copyright holders. Those to whom this applies are asked to contact us.

The map on page 48 was drawn by Peter Schmid.

DESTINATION CANYON COUNTRY
WINDSOR BOOKS INTERNATIONAL, 1992

© 1988 by Verlag C.J. Bucher GmbH, Munich and Berlin
Translation: Bradford Robinson
Editor: Karen Lemiski
Anthology: Carmel Finnan, Karen Lemiski